Alan Brown's Diary

Frederick L. Wolf

Alan Brown's Diary

Ernst Klett Sprachen
Stuttgart

Klett-Augmented-App kostenlos downloaden und öffnen

Bilderkennung starten und Titelseite (S. 3) scannen

Audios laden, scrollen direkt nutzen oder speichern

1. Auflage 1 15 14 13 | 2024 23 22 21

Nachfolger von 978-3-12-571450-2
Alle Drucke dieser Auflage sind unverändert und können im Unterricht nebeneinander verwendet werden.
Die letzte Zahl bezeichnet das Jahr des Druckes.

Internetadresse: www.klett-sprachen.de

Autor: Frederick L. Wolf
Das Lied auf S. 34 schrieb Wolfgang Froese, Oldenburg

Redaktion: Rona McGeoch, Bayreuth (diese Ausgabe)
Layoutkonzeption: Elmar Feuerbach
Gestaltung und Satz: Eva Mokhlis, Swabianmedia, Stuttgart
Umschlaggestaltung: Sandra Vrabec
Titelbild: shutterstock (SnowStock), New York, NY
Druck und Bindung: Plump Druck & Medien GmbH

Printed in Germany

ISBN 978-3-12-571452-6

9 783125 714526

Contents

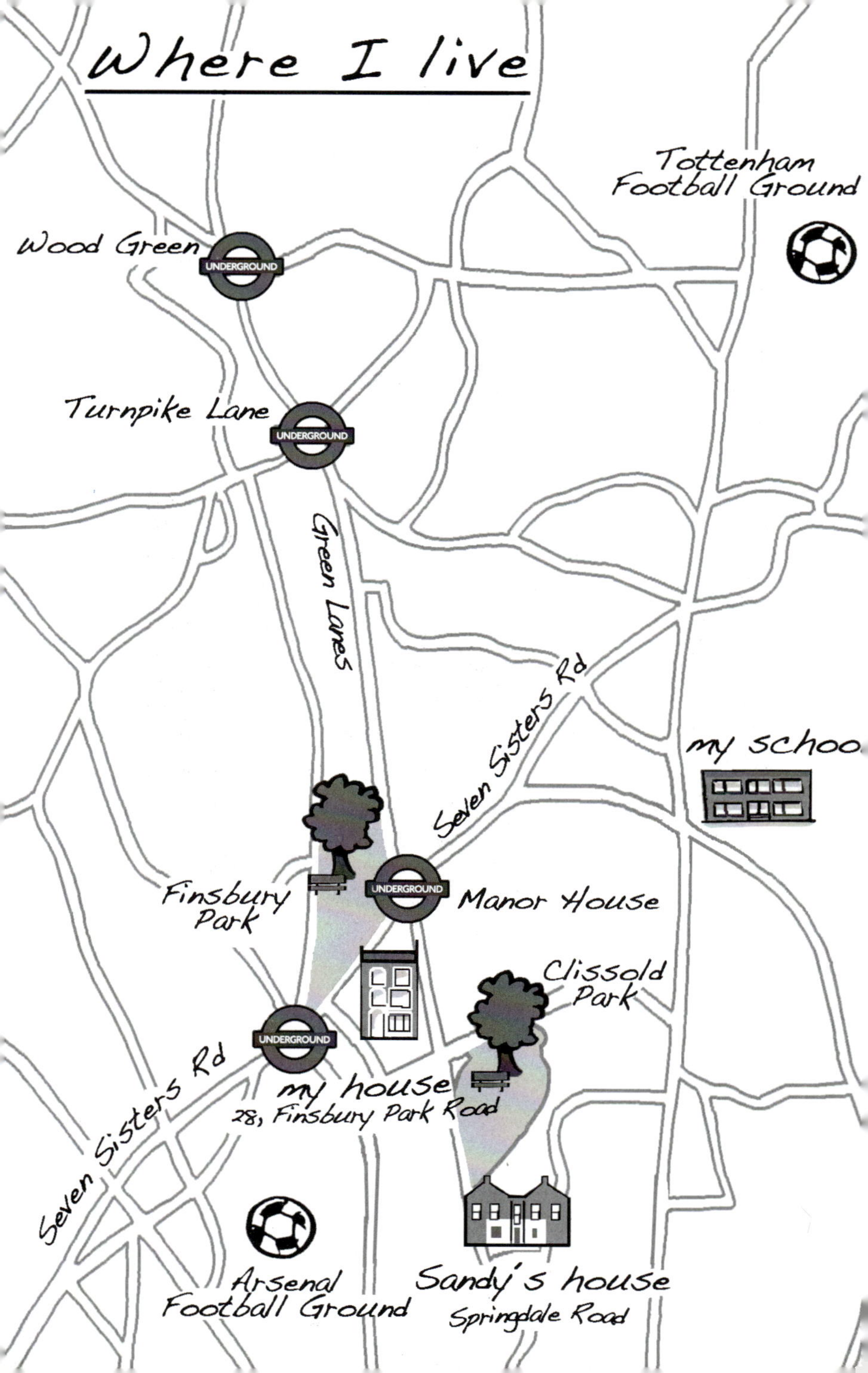
Where I live
Tottenham
Football Ground
Wood Green
UNDERGROUND
Turnpike Lane
UNDERGROUND
Green Lanes
Seven Sisters Rd
my schoo
Finsbury
Park
UNDERGROUND
Manor House
Clissold
Park
UNDERGROUND
Seven Sisters Rd
my house
28, Finsbury Park Road
Arsenal
Football Ground
Sandy's house
Springdale Road

My name is Alan Brown.
I live at 28, Finsbury Park Road, London N4.
My hobbies are football and pop music.
I'm also interested in girls.
My favourite subjects are Physical Education and Music.
I hate Geography, Maths and French.
My sister is 17 and stupid.
My mother is a housewife.
My father works away from home.

my school

Part I

Monday, September 24th

It was great at school today. There was a new girl in our class. Her name is Sandy and she's from Manchester. She moved to London with her family last weekend. She's fantastic. It's a pity that she doesn't sit next to me. She sits next to Kevin. How can she??? Kevin looks like a monkey.

I haven't talked to Sandy yet, but I'll try tomorrow.

Tuesday, September 25th

I couldn't speak to Sandy because she wasn't at school today. I don't know what happened to her. Perhaps she's ill. I couldn't follow the lessons because I was thinking of Sandy all the time. I hope she will be in school tomorrow.

Wednesday, September 26th

Sandy was there again. Ah! But I haven't spoken to her yet. I wanted to a few times, but I just couldn't do it. She has beautiful hair. I love it.

During the Geography lesson the teacher asked me, "What's the capital of Germany?" – I was dreaming of Sandy and her long red hair. It's wonderful. – The teacher shouted, "Alan, wake up! What's the capital of Germany?" I was still dreaming and so I said, "Long red hair." – Everybody was laughing. Only the teacher became very angry and shouted at me again. Mr Johnson shouts too much – I don't think it's good for him.

5 **it's a pity** es ist schade

It's ten o'clock in the evening now, and I'm watching an action film on TV. My mother has gone out and my sister won't be home until late. So I have the lounge all to myself. I'm a bit worried because I haven't learned my French vocabulary for tomorrow yet. Perhaps I can start when the film is over.

Thursday, September 27th

I was lucky! Our French teacher was ill today. We had a Biology lesson instead. We talked about insects. I wonder if insects can fall in love, too.

During the History lesson Brian threw bits of paper at Sandy all the time. It really made me angry. After the lesson I told Brian to keep his fingers off Sandy. Brian only laughed and showed off his big muscles ...

Friday, September 28th

TGIF!! (Thank God it's Friday!)

At last. I met Sandy in the school cafeteria during lunch break. I nearly dropped my plate of sausage and chips over her. I'm glad I didn't because she looked great in her new school uniform. I asked her, "Do you like it at our school?" She said, "NO!" I tried hard to smile at her but I think I looked too serious.

Brian said some dirty things about me at the lunch table. If he goes on like that he will get himself into trouble. My mother went out again. It's the second night this week that she has stayed out late. I wonder what she's doing!

9 **insect** ['ɪnsekt] Insekt – 10 **to fall in love** sich verlieben – 13 **to keep one's fingers off sb** jm in Ruhe lassen; die Finger davon lassen – 14 **he showed off his muscles** ['mʌslz] er ließ seine Muskeln spielen

Saturday, September 29th

I wanted to sleep in today. But the milkman rang the doorbell at seven o'clock. He wanted to tell us that the price of milk had gone up again. Why can't he do it on a school day?

I had a nice dream last night. I dreamed that I was walking hand in hand with Sandy through the streets of Manchester. She looked even more beautiful in jeans and a green top than in her new school uniform. She told me everything about her life and that she was in love with me. I wanted to tell her that I was in love with her, too. I wanted to kiss her, but then that stupid milkman rang the doorbell and woke me up. The dream was over.

Sunday, September 30th

I stayed in bed until 11 o'clock. When I came into the kitchen Mum was sitting at the kitchen table. Something was wrong. She hadn't brushed her hair and she had no make-up on. She usually puts her make-up on before breakfast. Her glasses were lying on the table and she was crying. She said, "I haven't heard from your father for a week now. I've tried to phone him but nobody answers the phone ..."

Monday, October 1st

I didn't sleep very well. I'm worried about Dad. He's working on an oil rig in the North Sea somewhere east of Scotland. I know that it can be a very hard and dangerous job. You can easily slip and break an arm or a leg or you can fall into the water and die when there's a storm. There could also be a fire or an explosion.

20 **glasses** (pl n) Brille

There was some kind of small "explosion" in my room. My computer doesn't work anymore. I don't know what's wrong with it.

Tuesday, October 2nd

The most fantastic thing happened to me today. During morning break Sandy asked me to help her with the French homework. I didn't know what to say, I was so surprised. I hope this means I will get a second chance.

Good news from my dad. He phoned us today to tell us that there had been a terrible storm in the North Sea and that they hadn't been able to telephone anybody. Now the storm is over and everything is back to normal. I wonder what life on an oil rig is like. It must be very boring. You can't go anywhere and you see the same people all the time.

Wednesday, October 3rd

I told my mother at breakfast that I want a guitar for Christmas. I want to be a pop star. My mother said that she wanted to talk about this with my father first. That's a good sign.

I saw a strange-looking man standing on the corner of the street when I came home from school. At seven o'clock he was still standing there.

Thursday, October 4th

I tried to write a little poem for Sandy, but I don't think it's good enough yet. I'll try again over the weekend.

My sister came home with a dog. It looks really funny. It's grey and white. It has long ears and a big

26 **poem** ['pəʊɪm] Gedicht

face. It's also quite fat. My sister likes it because of its beautiful brown eyes. She said that it had run after her all the way home from the tube station. My mother didn't want to take the dog in. So we put him up in the garden.

Friday, October 5th

Didn't sleep very well because the dog was barking in the garden all the time. At four o'clock in the morning we had to bring the dog inside because the neighbours began to shout at it to shut up. My mother put the dog in the kitchen.

At seven o'clock my mother got up. She went into the kitchen but the dog wasn't there. She found it in the lounge lying on the sofa. There was a funny smell. Mother became very angry. "The dog must go!", she

3 **tube station** [tju:b] U-Bahnstation – 10 **to shut up** die Schnauze halten – 14 **smell** Geruch

said. My sister started crying.[1] At eight o'clock my sister and the dog left the house.

When I came home from school the strange-looking man was there again. He waited at the corner for more than two hours.

It's ten o'clock in the evening now and my sister hasn't come home yet. Perhaps the dog has run away and she's looking for it.

Saturday, October 6th

I began to write a poem for Sandy:

I love your beautiful green eyes
and your long red hair is nice.

"That's really terrible. I give up for today," I shouted angrily. My sister phoned at lunchtime. She's staying with a friend. The dog is with her.

I went to see Arsenal play against Liverpool. It was a good game. Arsenal won 2-1. I'm not a real football fan. I only go there because most of my friends are there.

Wanted to look up Sandy on Facebook. But I can't get that stupid computer going again to get onto the Internet.

Sunday, October 7th

I had a nice breakfast with cornflakes, bacon and eggs, toast with marmalade, fruit juice and tea. During the week it's just cornflakes for breakfast, but today I wanted something special. It's a special day today. I've written the first love poem of my life. Here it is:

1 **she started crying** sie fing an zu weinen

Dear Sandy. In the sunshine, in the rain,
In cars, on buses, or on a train,
During the day and through the night,
In the dark or in sunlight,
I'll tell you one thing that is true,
The one I'm thinking of is
YOU!

Monday, October 8th

Went to school but it was closed. I forgot that the teachers have gone on strike for two days. They are asking for more money.

I was sad because I couldn't give my poem to Sandy. What would she think of it? What does she think of me? What does she think of the other boys in our class? Perhaps she has already got a boyfriend. My heart was beating quickly.

In the afternoon I played football in the park with some of the boys from our neighbourhood. I had to play in goal for most of the time. I didn't like it much because it was a cold and windy day and I was freezing. – When I left the park after the match the strange-looking man was there again.

My stupid sister is still staying with her friend. I hope her friend likes dogs. Perhaps my sister will stay there, just to keep the dog. A nice idea.

10 **to go on strike** [straɪk] streiken

Tuesday, October 9th

No school today. Brilliant! The teachers are still on strike. They want more money. – I want more money as well! But my mum doesn't want to give me any more pocket money. Perhaps I'll get a job as a newspaper boy. But then I would have to get up at six o'clock in the morning. Oh, well!

Wednesday, October 10th

Everything is back to normal. Before school I put my poem into the nicest envelope I could find. Later at school I waited for a chance to give the poem to Sandy. But I couldn't find the right moment. It was only after the last lesson when everybody was leaving the classroom that I was able to do it. In the corridor I walked right behind Sandy and then I put the envelope into her bag. I hope she'll find it there.

When I came home my sister was already there. That stupid dog was lying on my bed. I gave it a kick. My sister shouted at me, "Stop that! If you can get a guitar for Christmas I have the right to keep a dog." Then my mother came in. First she looked at me, then she looked at the dog and in the end she turned to my sister and said, "Wait until your father comes home. You know that I hate dogs." Then she left for Bingo.

It's late at night. I'm thinking of Sandy. Has she read my poem? What does she think of it?

2 **brilliant** [ˈbrɪljənt] toll, spitze – 14 **corridor** [ˈkɒrɪdɔː] Korridor, Gang – 15 **envelope** [ˈenvələʊp] Briefumschlag

Thursday, October 11th

We had a terrible night. I had only just fallen asleep when we were woken up by the fire-brigade. I think it was about 2 am. Our neighbours' house was on fire. There was a lot of smoke. A girl was crying. I couldn't see her. Then I saw Mr Miller, our neighbour, who was standing on the grass in front of his house. He shouted, "There she is!" – "Where?" Mrs Miller asked. "Look, there on the roof." – Judy, Mr and Mrs Miller's daughter, had climbed out of the window and onto the roof. An ambulance arrived and stopped in front of our house. A fireman climbed up a ladder to the roof of the house. He took the girl and carried her down to the ambulance. The ambulance drove away quickly. The firemen were able to put out the fire in about half an hour. At 3 am it was all over and we could go back to sleep.

At school I was very tired. I couldn't follow the lessons. Sandy didn't look at me once. I don't know whether she has read my poem or not.

Kevin and I had a little fight at lunchtime. I think he's in love with Sandy, too. Brian was standing in the corner. He was watching us and he was laughing loudly.

Friday, October 12th

Found a note under my desk at school. It said, "Keep your hands off Sandy or I'll hit you." That was all. No name. Nothing. I think Kevin wrote the note.

I went to a music shop after school and had a look at all the instruments. I think a keyboard will be better than a guitar. As a keyboard player it might be easier

9 **roof** [ruːf] Dach

to become a pop star. With a keyboard and a computer you can easily make your own music. So perhaps I can also get some good software for my computer and then I'll start with the pop business. Wow! Oh, I forgot. My computer is still broken. Somebody will have to fix it first.

Today the strange-looking man was there again. At 5 pm he met another man in a black Jaguar. They sat in the car and talked to each other. Twenty minutes later the other man got out of the car and went away. The strange-looking man waited in the car for a moment and then he drove away.

Saturday, October 13th

Wanted to see the Arsenal match against Chelsea. But my mum said that she wouldn't give me any more money if I wanted a guitar for Christmas. I told her that I had changed my mind and that I didn't want a guitar any more. After she had given me the money for the match I told her that I wanted a keyboard. Before she could throw things at me I quickly rushed out of the house.

I went round to Stephen's and we watched some music videos. Stephen likes British rap music – very loud! I prefer American rap music but I don't like that very much either.

We were just watching an exciting new rap video when Stephen's mum came in and shouted, "What the hell is that? Stop that noise!!"

Stephen became angry and shouted back "It's not too loud. It's only because you don't like this kind of music.

8 **Jaguar** ['dʒægjʊə] britisches Auto der Nobelklasse – 17 **to change one's mind** seine Meinung ändern

You only like Madonna and Sting." "Yeah," I said, "I played frisbee with a Madonna CD yesterday. That's what they are good for." Stephen's mother didn't know what to say. She closed the door and went away. Ten minutes later we heard a strange noise. It came from the lounge. Stephen's mother had put on the vacuum-cleaner. Stephen switched off the TV and wanted to show me a new computer game, but I had to leave because of the football match.

The match was not too bad. But after the game I fell down the stairs and almost broke my nose. Now my nose is swollen.

Sunday, October 14th

Woke up with a headache. I went to the bathroom and had a look in the mirror. It was terrible. My nose was red and blue and it was very big.

I didn't go out today. I stayed in the lounge all day long and watched TV.

Monday, October 15th

Wanted to stay at home but my mother didn't want to write a note for school. My nose looked even worse. It had turned blue and green. I looked like a monster.

At school it was terrible. Everybody was laughing. Even our Geography teacher. At lunch break Sandy came up to me and said that she felt sorry for me. That made my day.

I'm quite happy now. There is still hope for a happy ending to this story.

6 **vacuum cleaner** Staubsauger – 25 **that made my day** das machte mich glücklich für den Rest des Tages

Tuesday, October 16th

Went to the shops down at Wood Green. I wanted to buy a present for Sandy, but I had no idea what to buy. I walked around for over two hours. It really drove me crazy. In the end I had a hamburger with chips and went back to the underground station.

Back home I saw the strange-looking man again. He was wearing a funny old beige raincoat and a black cap. I must find out why he's waiting at the corner almost every day.

My mum has gone out again. She goes out almost every evening. I don't know where she's going and she doesn't want to tell me.

Wednesday, October 17th

Sandy told me that she liked my poem. At last!!!!!! I asked her if she would like to sit next to me during lessons. She said that she wanted to sit next to Kevin because he's very good at most subjects.

When I came home my sister was crying. The dog had been run over by a London transport bus. The dog had to be taken to the vet's. The vet had to operate on the dog and it's not yet clear whether the dog will live.

Thursday, October 18th

My dad phoned this morning. He'll be coming home for a few days next week. I'm looking forward to that. I'll ask him about his work on the oil rig. Perhaps one day I can work there, too, and earn a lot of money.

Kevin is having a party on Saturday. I don't know whether Sandy will be there, too. So I must go to the party and find out.

21 **vet** Tierarzt – 21 **to operate on** ['ɒpəreɪt] operieren

Friday, October 19th

Sad news from the vet. The dog is dead. My sister stayed in her room all day long and cried her eyes out.

Tomorrow is Kevin's party and I still don't know what to wear. What kind of clothes does Sandy like???

Saturday, October 20th

No time for the diary today. I must get ready for the party. It's important.

Sunday, October 21st

I'm sad. Sandy wasn't there. In fact there were no girls at all. There were only Kevin and his Arsenal supporters. Kevin's parents were away for the evening. They had gone out to see a new musical in the Westend. The party was boring – I left at half past nine. – Must try to get Sandy's phone number. She has a little red mobile. Really cool.

Monday, October 22nd

During morning break some of the girls were standing together with Brian. They were looking at a photo on Brian's mobile. It was a photo of Theo Walcott, the England striker. The girls love him.

14 **Westend** Londoner Innenstadt, wo sich die großen Theater und Kaufhäuser befinden

Back home I saw the strange-looking man again. This time he was sitting on a park bench talking to a good-looking woman for more than an hour. He must be a spy or something. I was just passing by when he got on a bus. So I jumped on as well. I wanted to find out where he was going. He got off at Turnpike Lane tube station and went down the High Road towards Wood Green. He was walking fast and I could hardly follow him. Suddenly I noticed something behind a shop window. I couldn't believe my eyes. It was my mother. She was cleaning the floors. Now I knew where she went almost every night. I walked on but the strange-looking man wasn't there anymore. So I took the next bus home. – I hope my mum didn't see me. She told me not to walk around North London after dark. It can be dangerous.

Tuesday, October 23rd

Brian invited Sandy to go to a football match at Spurs', but Sandy said "No". – Why did she do that? Maybe she's not interested in football. I only hope that she's not interested in Brian.

Wednesday, October 24th

My dad arrived in the afternoon. He had grown a beard and looked a bit like Father Christmas. He asked me questions about school. I didn't tell him that I was in love with Sandy.

I asked him what life was like on the oil rig. He said, "Well, it's not funny. We sometimes work sixteen hours

2 **bench** [ˈbentʃ] Bank – 3 **good-looking** gutaussehend – 4 **spy** [spaɪ] Spion – 18 **Spurs** [spɜːz] Kurzform für Tottenham Hotspurs, der zweite große Fußballverein im Norden Londons – 23 **beard** [ˈbɪəd] Bart

a day. The weather is bad most of the time and I have to work outside quite often. The people on the oil rig aren't very friendly. They are only there for the money. The only good thing is the food."

Thursday, October 25th

Mum and Dad went out in the late afternoon. So I had the lounge all to myself. I wanted to watch the telly but there was nothing on. So I looked out of the window instead and what did I see? The strange-looking man was talking to two other men who also looked very strange.

I decided to find out about those men. I went outside and followed them into the park. The men were walking towards the lake. When I got there I couldn't see them anymore. "Where are they?" I asked myself. – As it was almost dark outside I couldn't see much. I walked around the park for about ten minutes. I almost wanted to give up when I heard a noise right behind me. I turned round and looked straight into the face of a man.

It was the strange-looking man ...

7 **telly** Kurzform für TV

Part II

3 weeks later

Thursday, November 15th

I think it's about time I gave you some more information about the people in this diary.

My mother

Name	Jane
Age	35
Job	housewife, part-time cleaning lady
Hobbies	Bingo, Sudoko, watching telly
Height	168 cm
Weight	66 kilos
Hair	brown
Eyes	brown

My father

Name	James (Jim for short)
Age	38
Job	electrician
Height	Dad says "seven feet and two inches', but this can't be true
Weight	about 90 kilos
Hobbies	cricket (in summer), reading the Sunday paper (in winter)

3 **it's about time** es wird langsam Zeit – 8 **part-time** Teilzeit

Hair	not much left
Eyes	blue

My sister

Name	Susan (Susie for short)
Age	17 and a half
Job	wants to become a secretary
Height	170 cm
Weight	top secret
Eyes	greenish brown
Hair	changes every week, pink just now
Hobbies	animals, riding horses (but she hasn't got a horse)

Sandy

Name	Sandra Alice Cooper
Age	14
Height	168 cm
Weight	about 55 kilos
Eyes	I dare not look
Hair	long, red
Hobbies	reading music magazines, dancing, listening to all kinds of music
Favourite food	chicken wraps, chocolate muffins

10 **pink** rosa, pink – 18 **I dare not look** [deə] Ich traue mich nicht hinzuschauen

Brian

Name	Brian James Coldwell
Age	15
Height	173 cm
Weight	over 80 kilos. FAT!!!!
Hair	black
Eyes	very small
Hobbies	football
Favourite food	burgers, pakoras

Kevin

Name	Kevin Smith
Age	14 3/4
Height	166 cm
Weight	less than 60 kilos (THIN
Hair	dirty blond
Eyes	I don't know what colour
Hobbies	computer games
Favourite food	fish and chips

The strange-looking man

Name	I call him "Sherlock Holmes"
Age	about 45
Height	taller than Brian, but not as tall as my father

9 **pakora** [pə'kɔːrə] frittierter Gemüsesnack aus Indien

Weight	not more than 70 kilos
Hair	you can't see his hair because he always wears a cap
Eyes	blue (I think)
Clothes	he always wears an old beige raincoat
Hobbies	hanging around our street
Job	?????

Friday, November 16th

My mother allowed me to watch television all evening. I forgot the diary. Sorry!

Saturday, November 17th

My mother, my sister and I went shopping in Wood Green. My sister bought a pink top. I got some new shoes which I don't like *at* all. My mother looked at all kinds of things, but didn't buy anything.

Sunday, November 18th

The weather was very bad. It rained all day. My mother told me to tidy up my room. I found some old photos. My parents really looked good when they were young. My dad even had lots of hair then, too.

I also found a piece of paper. It was a page from my diary which I had thrown away angrily. It said:

Oct 25th: … The strange-looking man looked at me and said, "What are you doing here? It's too late for a little boy like you to be running around the park in the

5 **beige** [beɪʒ] beige – 5 **raincoat** ['reɪnkəʊt] Regenmantel

evening," I didn't know what to say; so I ran away. I ran straight home and went to my room. "Little boy!" that man had said. I'm not a little boy. I'm almost 15 (in words: F I F T E E N !).

Monday, November 19th

Too much homework today. No time for the diary.

Tuesday, November 20th

My dad is back on holiday. He doesn't want to work on the oil rig any more. He says it's too boring, too lonely and too dangerous. He will try to find another job near London.

My sister said, "We don't even know where you are working at the moment. We only know that it's an oil rig in the North Sea. And now you want to work in another place?" "Shut up, Susie," Dad said. "Susie is right," I said, "Where is that oil rig you're working on?" "Well," Dad said, "it is in the Brent oil field north-east of Scotland, if you know where that is. And now leave me alone."

Wednesday, November 21st

Sandy wore lipstick today. I wonder why she did that? School was boring. Too much homework again.

After dinner my father and I sat in my room. He looked at all the pictures of different pop stars on the wall. Then he asked me, "Do you have a girlfriend?" I said, "I don't know yet. Perhaps I'll have one soon." I asked my dad how he got to know Mum. He said that he had met her at the school dance. Suddenly my mother came in and started to laugh. "I remember," she said. "I had to ask you to dance with me. You were too shy." "Yes, I know," my father said, "I didn't want to dance at all. But it wasn't so bad."

Thursday, November 22nd

I didn't go to school this morning. I had to go to the dentist. He gave me two fillings. Ow! Perhaps I shouldn't eat so many sweets.

When I went back to school at lunchtime I saw Kevin in the toilet. He was smoking. I know Sandy hates people who smoke. If Sandy finds out that Kevin smokes, he'll be out of the race for Sandy.

Friday, November 23rd

Did quite well in the French test. Perhaps I'm starting to like French after all. I stood behind the kitchen door and listened to what Mum and Dad were saying:

Mum: When do you go back to work, Jim?

Dad: On Sunday evening. I'll take the night train to Aberdeen and in the morning I'll fly over to the oil rig.

2 **lipstick** Lippenstift – 12 **shy** [ˈʃaɪ] schüchtern – 16 **dentist** [ˈdentɪst] Zahnarzt – 16 **filling** Füllung – 21 **race** [ˈreɪs] Rennen

Mum: Will it be the last time that you have to go back?

Dad: I hope so. If I get that job in Norwich, I'll never go back to the oil rig again.

Mum: Do you think the kids and I should move to Norwich, too?

Dad: That wouldn't be a bad idea. We could at least be together all the time.

Saturday, November 24th

I didn't sleep at all last night. NORWICH! Oh no ... I hope my dad doesn't get the job there. That would be the end.

Sunday, November 25th

A lovely sunny day. Probably the last sunny day of the year. I went jogging in Clissold Park. Later I sat on a park bench where I met "Sherlock Holmes".

Sherlock: Hi, kid.

Me: Hello.

Sherlock: Haven't I seen you before?

Me: Yes. – You called me a "little boy," but I'm almost 15.

Sherlock (laughed): I can see that. Tell me, why were you following me the last time I saw you?

Me: Well, I wanted to find out who you were.

Sherlock: OK. I'll tell you.
I'm a police inspector and we are looking for some drug dealers.

29 **drug dealer** [ˌdrʌgˈdiːlə] Drogenhändler

Me: Have you found them yet?
Sherlock: No.

That was all the police inspector said. – Then he went away.

Monday, November 26th

Worked hard for the Maths test. I'm sure Sandy will like me if I'm good at Maths.

Brian wore a football T-shirt under his school uniform. He was sent home and had to put his normal shirt and tie on.

When I saw Sandy I couldn't believe my eyes. What had happened to her? She looked strange. Then I noticed. Her hair, – her beautiful long red hair, – it wasn't there anymore. Now her hair was very short. Oh no!

Tuesday, November 27th

I went to school early. Sandy was there, too. I told her I had met a police inspector who was looking for some drug dealers.

Me: Do you think anybody takes drugs at our school?
Sandy: I don't know.
Me: I saw a film about drugs on television the other night. It was terrible.
Sandy: My sister is 21 and she once had a boyfriend who took drugs. It was so sad. One day they had to take him to hospital. A few weeks later he died.

10 **tie** [taɪ] Schlips, Krawatte – 20 **drugs** Drogen

Me: It's terrible that young people die just because drug dealers want to make a lot of money.

Wednesday, November 28th

Mr Roberts, our Geography teacher, has given us some really stupid homework. For the next four weeks we'll have to look at the moon every night and find out what it looks like. It's really stupid because it'll be cloudy the whole time and you won't be able to see the moon anyway.

Thursday, November 29th

During Assembly the headmaster said that this year's school disco will be held on Friday, December 14th.

Friday, November 30th

The girls were talking about the school disco for most of the day. The boys didn't really know what to say. Most of them hate dancing.

Saturday, December 1st

Met "Sherlock Holmes" in the street outside our school.

Me: Any news from the drug dealers?
Sherlock: No. But you can keep your eyes open and tell me if you see anything.

Wow! I'm not "little boy" any more. Now I'm Sherlock's assistant. Just call me Dr Watson.

Sunday, December 2nd

A rainy day. In the afternoon I lay on my bed and dreamed about the future.

23 DAYS TILL CHRISTMAS!!! Will I get the keyboard? Will I be able to become a pop star? If I were a pop star I could get any girl I wanted ...

Monday, December 3rd

A letter from a company in Norwich arrived today. What will it say??? I don't want to live in Norwich. I want to stay in London. All my friends are here and, of course,

*S*A*N*D*Y*

Tuesday, December 4th

Haven't found anybody yet who is taking drugs at our school. Perhaps I'm just too blind to see it. Sandy hasn't been of much help either. She and all the other girls in my form are only talking about the school disco.

Wednesday, December 5th

Saw two young men in jeans and leather jackets outside the school. They were talking to some older pupils. Perhaps they're selling drugs. I'll find out about it ...

Brian had his hair cut: very short at the back and at the sides, like Theo Walcott. He looks like a bulldog now.

Thursday, December 6th

Great news! I finally got Sandy's phone number. –

20 **leather** ['leðə] Leder

Mum and Dad came home with a big parcel today. I hope that it's my Christmas present (the keyboard)!

Dad wasn't very happy. He only has a free weekend and must return to the oil rig on Monday – yet again. The company in Norwich won't decide about his job before the beginning of January. So that gives me a little bit of time.

Friday, December 7th

Sandy was very quiet today. At lunchtime I saw the reason why. She had been to the dentist. Now she's wearing a brace on her teeth. I didn't know what to say. I'm also not sure what I think of it.

Kevin is wearing an earring in his left ear. Ugh!! During the French lesson I had to read aloud. My voice sounded funny. I think it's finally breaking – at last! I'm finally becoming a MAN!!!!

Saturday, December 8th

Wrote the first song of my life:

1. Is it difficult to be young?
   Will this little song ever be sung?
   Will I be rich or will I be poor?
   I'll never live in Norwich, that's for sure.
2. Will I travel 'round the world?
   Will I find a beautiful girl?
   Will I ever be a man,
   Or will I just be a football fan?

Chorus: I have many questions. Who gives me the answers?

11 **brace** [breɪs] Zahnklammer – 15 **finally** ['faɪnəlɪ] endlich

I've tried to sing the song all afternoon, but it's very hard for me because my voice only makes funny noises.

Sunday, December 9th

Read an article in the *Sunday Mirror*:

Police inspector hurt in gun battle with drug dealers.

There was also a photo showing a police inspector in an ambulance. He looked a lot like "Sherlock Holmes" ...

6 **gun battle** [ˈgʌnˌbætl] Feuergefecht

Monday, December 10th

Spoke to Sandy about Sherlock. I didn't say much because my voice keeps breaking all the time. Sandy didn't say much either. I think she's having problems with her brace.

Tuesday, December 11th

My sister is growing up, too. This time she didn't bring a dog home – this time it was her new boyfriend. My mother says that he's much too old for her. But I think he only looks about nineteen or so. He's got very short black hair, big ears and a small nose. I wonder where Susie found him?

Wednesday, December 12th

Steve (Susie's boyfriend) was here again. I hope he doesn't stay any longer than the dog did. At least he doesn't bark at night.

Thursday, December 13th

Tried to phone Sandy, but she didn't answer the phone. I wonder why? – School disco tomorrow. Will it be an important day in my life? Just think of my parents!!

Friday, December 14th

Brian wasn't at school today. I hope he's ill and can't come to the disco. I went home straight after school and had a little rest on the sofa. I didn't feel very well.

School disco started at 7 pm. I couldn't see Brian. Thank God. Kevin had another ring in his left ear. What does he need two rings in his ear for? One ring is ugly enough!

Sandy arrived five minutes after I did. She looked great in her new black jeans, leather boots and a green sweatshirt.

She talked to the French teacher for quite a long time. Then she went to dance with some of the girls from our form. I stood by the wall most of the time and watched Sandy. She didn't look at me once.

After the disco I saw Sandy standing at the bus stop. "Where have you been all evening?" she asked. "Oh, around," I answered. I didn't know what else to say. We stood there waiting for more than 20 minutes, but no bus turned up. "I think we've missed the last bus. Let's walk, shall we?" said Sandy. "Can I walk you home?" I asked. "That would be great," she said.

We didn't talk much on the way to Sandy's house. When we arrived there I wanted to kiss her but I was too nervous. I just said "See you on Monday," turned around and started to leave. Then Sandy said, "I'm going to the cinema next week. Would you like to come with me?" "Wow, I'd love to," I shouted. "See you!" Then I ran off.

Saturday, December 15th

Oh, what a happy day!!!!!!!!!!!

Sunday, December 16th

Watched Manchester United against Arsenal on TV. Not a good match. No goals.

1 **ugly** [ˈʌglɪ] häßlich – 14 **to turn up** auftauchen, erscheinen

Monday, December 17th

Dad phoned up. He doesn't want to stay on the oil rig any longer. There was a terrible storm and he was frightened. I'm a bit worried about him, too. He's not a very good swimmer.

Sandy told me that she wanted to go to the cinema on Wednesday at 6 pm, if that would be all right with me. I'd go any time or anywhere, if she asked me!

Tuesday, December 18th

While I was doing my homework, I could hear Susie and my mother in the lounge. They were talking about problems. I could only understand that it was about Susie's boyfriend and drugs. This could be important. Perhaps I can find out more about it ...

Wednesday, December 19th

Went to the cinema with Sandy. It was wonderful.

Thursday, December 20th

I think I'm in love for the first time in my life. What a feeling! Life is great!

Friday, December 21st

Last day of school before Christmas. Sad news for me. Sandy told me that she would go to Scotland with her parents over Christmas. So I won't be able to see her for the next two weeks.

Perhaps I should write another song, this time about love and loneliness.

26 **loneliness** ['ləʊnlɪnɪs] Einsamkeit

Saturday, December 22nd

Stayed in bed until 12 o'clock. I don't know whether I'm happy or sad.

Dad came home. He's not going back to the oil rig. Mum arrived with another big parcel. Susie's boyfriend was arrested by the police.

Sunday, December 23rd

A quiet day. Nothing happened.

Monday, December 24th

I woke up at 5 o'clock in the morning. A lot of questions came to my mind:

Will Sandy be my girlfriend?
What will Brian do?
Will Kevin still be my best friend?
Will our family move to another place when Dad gets a new job?
Will Susie get a new dog or a new boyfriend?
What about the drug dealers?
Will "Sherlock Holmes" get out of hospital soon?
Will I get my keyboard tomorrow?
Will I become a pop star?

All these questions, and tomorrow is

CHRISTMAS!!!

11 **to come to one's mind** einem in den Sinn kommen

Exercises

1 Is it right (r), wrong (w) or just silly (s)?

		r	w	s
1.	Alan likes Geography, Maths and French.			
2.	Sandy is from Newcastle.			
3.	On Oct. 3rd, a girl was standing on the corner of a street.			
4.	Susan likes dogs.			
5.	Arsenal flies over Clissold Park.			
6.	Theo Walcott is a singer.			
7.	Sandy is smaller than Susan.			
8.	Mrs Brown works in Norwich.			
9.	Good-looking dentists eat music magazines.			
10.	Alan loves Sandy.			

2 A crossword

1. Girls put it on. 2. Alan tried to write it. 3. You put a letter into it. 4. He gives you fillings. 5. Boots are made of it. 6. A colour. 7. Everybody has it. 8. You can sit on it. 9. The teachers at Alan's school went on it. 10. A person.

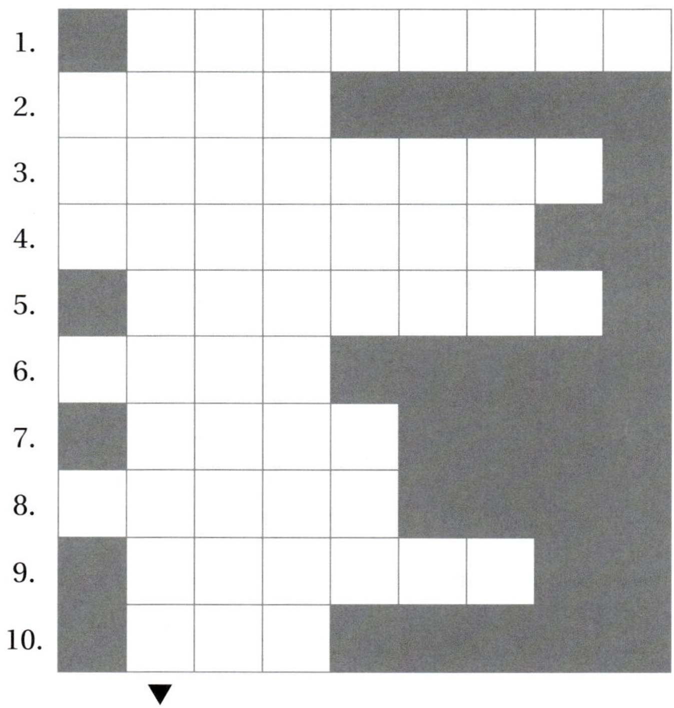

Most people are afraid of it: ______________________

3 Favourites

	Alan	You
subjects		
hobbies		
pop group		
football team		
interests		
friends		
colour		

4 Problems

Do you have the same problems as Alan? Put an X.

		Yes	No
1.	I want to have a girl/boyfriend.		
2.	I want to have a lot of friends.		
3.	I want to become a pop star.		
4.	My sister/brother gets on my nerves.		
5.	I'd like to sleep long.		
6.	I hate Maths.		
7.	I'm a bit shy.		
8.	I think that I'm not good-looking.		
9.	My father is away from home most of the time.		
10.	I don't have enough money.		

5 A Test

Do you want to be a pop star? – Test yourself.
Put an X.

		Yes	No	Don't know
1.	Do you want to have many good friends?			
2.	Can you play an instrument?			
3.	Do you want to have a private life?			
4.	Are you good-looking?			
5.	Do you sometimes hate yourself?			
6.	Are you a good singer?			
7.	Do you find it difficult to speak in front of the class?			
8.	Do you like to sleep in hotel beds?			
9.	Do you want to have a good family life?			
10.	Would you like to play in a school band?			

Auswertung 2 Punkte bekommst du für jedes „yes“ bei allen Fragen mit gerader Zahl und für jedes „no“ bei den Fragen mit ungerader Zahl. Für alle anderen Antworten erhältst du 0 Punkte.

6 Looking into the future

What do you think of Alan's questions at the end of his diary? Can you give him any answers?

7 Rhyme time

Try to write a song or poem about love and loneliness.

8 Writing

Alan would like to write an e-mail to Sandy while she's away in Scotland, but he's not quite sure. Can you help him? You can start like this:

> Hi Sandy,
>
> 7 more days until you come back to London.
>
> ____________ lonely without ____________
>
> ____________ Christmas ____________ Christmas
>
> presents ____________ ____________ keyboard
>
> ____________ Susie ____________ ____________
>
> Kevin ____________ TV ____________ football
>
> ____
>
> Love,
>
> Alan

Answers

1 1.w|2.w|3.w|4.r|5.s|6.w|7.r|8.w|9.s|10?

2

		L	I	P	S	T	I	C	K
	P	**O**	E	M					
	E	**N**	V	E	L	O	P	E	
	D	**E**	N	T	I	S	T		
		L	E	A	T	H	E	R	
	P	**I**	N	K					
		N	A	M	E				
	B	**E**	N	C	H				
		S	T	R	I	K	E		
		S	P	Y					

3 (for Alan): 1. Physical Education, Music 2. football, pop music 3. -- 4. Arsenal 5. girls 6. Sandy, Kevin, Stephen 7. red

5 ***More than 16 points***

You can become a pop star if you really want to.

10-16 points

You can make it, but you will have to work very hard for it.

6-9 points

Don't worry, be happy. But not as a pop star. Perhaps you could become a roady or a groupy.

0-5 points

No chance. Try to play tennis or do something else.

Bildquellennachweis

6 Sven Palmowski, Barcelona; **7** Alamy Images (Chris Gascoigne), Abingdon, Oxon; **12** Thinkstock (Hemera), München; **20** Corbis (EXPA/David Rawcliffe/NewSport), Düsseldorf; **27** shutterstock (Yvan), New York, NY; **34** Helga Merkle, Zell; **38** shutterstock (vnlit), New York, NY

Sollte es einmal nicht gelungen sein, den korrekten Rechteinhaber ausfindig zu machen, so werden berechtigte Ansprüche selbstverständlich im Rahmen der üblichen Regelungen abgegolten. Die Positionsangabe der Bilder erfolgt je Seite von oben nach unten, von links nach rechts.